Sports Illustrated KIDS

STARS OF SPORTS

JAMES HARDEN

BASKETBALL SHARPSHOOTER

by Matt Chandler

CAPSTONE PRESS
a capstone imprint

Stars of Sports is published by
Capstone Press, an imprint of Capstone
1710 Roe Crest Drive, North Mankato, Minnesota 56003
www.capstonepub.com

Library of Congress Cataloging-in-Publication Data
Names: Chandler, Matt, author.
Title: James Harden : basketball sharpshooter / Matt Chandler.
Description: North Mankato, Minnesota : Captivate is published by Capstone Press, [2021] | Series: SIK Stars of Sports | Includes bibliographical references and index. | Audience: Ages 8-11 years | Audience: Grades 4-6 |
Summary: "James Harden was a top pick in the 2012 NBA draft, but he wasn't an instant superstar. Harden worked tirelessly to improve his skill. His dedication paid off, both for him and the Houston Rockets. Harden is now one of the best players in the league. Readers will learn how James Harden used determination and hard work to take him to the top!"— Provided by publisher.
Identifiers: LCCN 2021002827 (print) | LCCN 2021002828 (ebook) | ISBN 9781663907196 (Hardcover) | ISBN 9781663907165 (PDF) | ISBN 9781663907189 (Kindle Edition)
Subjects: LCSH: Harden, James, 1989—-Juvenile literature. | Basketball players—United States—Biography—Juvenile literature. | Arizona State University—Basketball—History. | Basketball—United States—History—Juvenile literature. | National Basketball Association—History—Juvenile literature.
Classification: LCC GV884.H2435 C53 2021 (print) | LCC GV884.H2435 (ebook) | DDC 796.323092 [B]—dc23
LC record available at https://lccn.loc.gov/2021002827
LC ebook record available at https://lccn.loc.gov/2021002828

Editorial Credits
Editor: Mandy Robbins; Designer: Dina Her; Media Researcher: Morgan Walters; Production Specialist: Tori Abraham

Image Credits
Associated Press: Bahram Mark Sobhani, 5, George Frey, 17, Jason DeCrow, 14, Mary Altaffer, 28; Getty Images: Allen Berezovsky, 6; Newscom: AJ Mast/Icon SMI, 9, Brian Rothmuller/Icon Sportswire DHZ, cover, Elmar Kremser/SVEN SIMON/picture alliance, 19, GEORGE FREY/EFE, 24, Javier Rojas/ZUMA Press, 27, JC Olivera/ Sipa USA, 22, LUCAS JACKSON/REUTERS, 15, Matt A. Brown/Icon SMI, 11, 12; Shutterstock: Oleksii Sidorov, 1; Sports Illustrated: John W. McDonough, 13, 16, 21, 23

All internet sites appearing in back matter were available and accurate when this book was sent to press.

TABLE OF CONTENTS

Words in **BOLD** are in the glossary.

A TOUGH COMPETITOR

Arizona Sun Devils star James Harden was thrilled to be picked by the Oklahoma City Thunder as the third pick in the 2009 National Basketball Association (NBA) Draft. Top draft picks are expected to be starters right away. But unlike 2009 picks Steph Curry and Blake Griffin, Harden didn't start a single game in his **rookie** season.

Other players might have struggled going from being a college superstar to a bench player. Not Harden. He studied the game and learned from his teammates.

"Being drafted the third overall pick, most guys would come in and think they're going to be a starter on any team," Harden said. "Scotty [former Oklahoma City Thunder coach Scott Brooks] did a great job of making me become that sixth man off the bench."

》》》 Harden goes up for a dunk over San Antonio Spurs guard Manu Ginobili.

FACT

A team's "sixth man" is the bench player that the coach most often subs in first for one of the starting players.

James Edward Harden Jr. was born in Los Angeles, California, on August 26, 1989. He was the youngest of three children. Harden and his brother and sister were raised by a single mother. His mom, Monja, worried Harden might join a gang. She pushed him to play sports. She hoped it would keep him out of trouble.

〉〉〉 Harden poses with his family at the 2018 NBA Awards.

Today, Harden is a superstar on the basketball court. But as a child, he actually chose to play baseball. "He played baseball for three or four years," his mom said. "Then he came to me and said he was ready for basketball." At that point, her son fell in love with the game. "He told me, 'I'm going to be an NBA player!'" she said.

Southpaw Success

As a young boy, Harden's first sport was baseball. He was a left-handed pitcher. He also played first base. When asked if he was good at baseball, Harden once described himself as "a little Randy Johnson." Johnson is a Hall of Fame pitcher who spent more than 20 years in the major leagues.

Today, Harden still enjoys baseball. He loves the game so much he goes to games by himself!

HIGH SCHOOL HOOPS

Harden's dad spent a lot of time in jail. During Harden's childhood, his dad wasn't around to teach him how to play basketball or anything else. Harden had to teach himself.

"I would just go out in our driveway and shoot," he said. "I'd be out there 'til 1:30–2 in the morning, just shooting."

That hard work paid off. Harden became the only freshman to make his **varsity** team. He played at Artesia High School, in Lakewood, California, just outside of Los Angeles.

Harden was a great shooter, but he wasn't the best athlete. He suffered from **asthma**. He worked hard on his fitness so he could keep up with other players. People doubted him, but Harden didn't doubt himself.

"I felt like I was going to be a star one day," he said. "I didn't know when, but I knew one day it would happen."

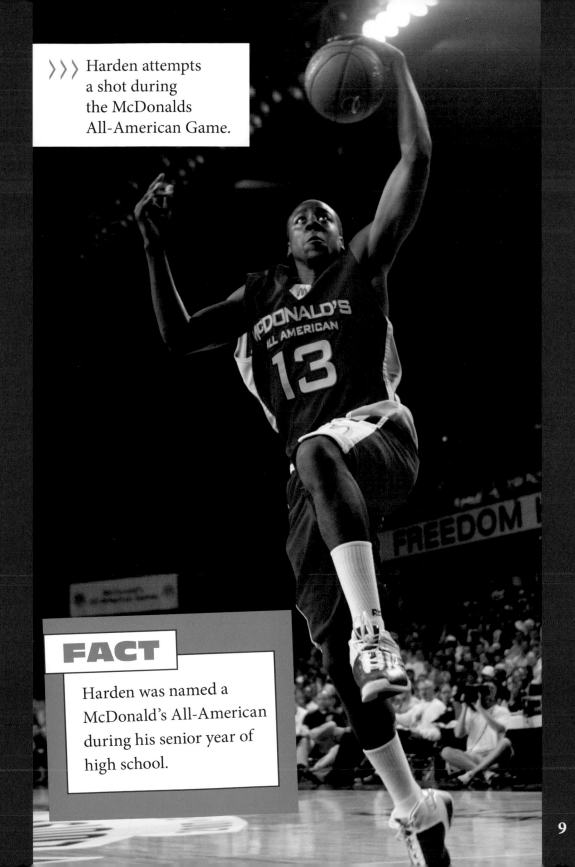

>>> Harden attempts a shot during the McDonalds All-American Game.

FACT

Harden was named a McDonald's All-American during his senior year of high school.

CHAPTER TWO

SUN DEVIL SUPERSTAR

Harden finished his high school career by leading Artesia High to back-to-back state championships in 2005–06 and 2006–07. Harden was **recruited** by many colleges. They included the University of California in Los Angeles (UCLA), North Carolina State University, and Arizona State University. His high school coach took a job at Arizona State. Harden followed him. The kid from Los Angeles who grew up shooting hoops in his driveway was now a Sun Devil!

On November 19, 2007, Harden played his first college game. It was against the University of Illinois. Though he started the game, he didn't play very well. He made just two of the nine shots he attempted. He added two free throws to finish the game with six points. The Sun Devils lost 77–54.

〉〉〉 Harden takes a shot while playing for Arizona State in 2008.

But things soon changed. The team won its next four games, with Harden scoring 20 points per game. He led his team to a record of 21–13. That was good enough to land a spot in the 2008 National Invitation Tournament (NIT).

Arizona State didn't win the championship. But Sun Devil fans were already looking forward to a second season with their young superstar.

Harden got even better in his second season at Arizona. He led the team, averaging 20 points per game. He started all 35 games.

Harden's best game of the season came against the University of Texas El Paso (UTEP) in the 76 Classic tournament. He led his team with 40 points. He made six shots from three-point range.

〉〉〉 Harden celebrates during a Sun Devils game in 2008.

The biggest moment came late in the fourth quarter. Arizona State led by 27 points. They were sure to win. In celebration, Harden took a bounce pass from teammate Jerren Shipp. He glided down court and delivered a thundering dunk!

〉〉〉 Harden rocks the beard during it's early stages in 2010.

The Beard Is Born

Harden's nickname is "The Beard." His bushy beard has made him almost as famous as his shooting. He first began to grow the beard in college. He has said he wanted to look older. He also admits he just didn't want to shave. Then he decided he liked the look.

DECISION DAY

After two seasons, Harden made the decision to leave Arizona State for the NBA. Staying in college could mean risking an injury and losing his chance to play as a pro one day. Playing in the NBA meant a contract worth millions of dollars.

"It's a dream come true," Harden said at the time. "It's my dream since I put a ball in my hand, so why not take the opportunity?"

Harden played very well when the top college players in the country came together at the 2009 **NBA Combine**. He was strong, fast, and he could jump. It was enough to have many experts say he would be drafted in the top five.

FACT

Harden was drafted four spots ahead of Golden State superstar Steph Curry in the 2009 NBA Draft.

>>> Harden shakes hands with NBA commissioner David Stern after being drafted by the Oklahoma City Thunder.

Harden was the third pick in the 2009 Draft. On June 25, 2009, the Oklahoma City Thunder chose him. Harden signed a two-year contract with the Thunder worth $4.76 million!

CHAPTER THREE

OFF TO OKLAHOMA

On October 28, 2009, Harden made his NBA debut. He didn't start the game. But he did play 13 minutes. He finished his first game with five points. Harden's rookie season began quietly. Harden believed he was good enough to be a starting guard. It was hard for him to go from being a superstar in Arizona to watching from the sidelines in Oklahoma City. "I came off the bench, so once again I just had to be humble and just continue to work," he said.

〉〉〉 Harden shoots a free throw during Game Two of the 2012 NBA Finals.

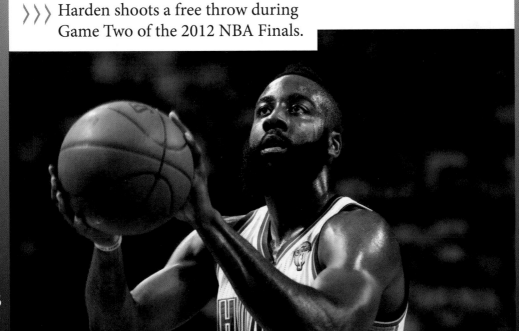

He did continue to work, and it paid off. He didn't start a single game in his rookie season. Still, Harden averaged nearly 10 points a game and helped the Thunder reach the playoffs.

〉〉〉 Harden beats the Utah Jazz's Carlos Boozer to the basket during a 2009 game.

SIXTH MAN

By his second season, Harden was used to his role. At one point, his coach offered to make him a starter.

"I said no," Harden said. "We had a chemistry. My role was to come off the bench and that was for the better of the team."

Along with Kevin Durant and Russell Westbrook, Harden made the Thunder a powerhouse. By his third season in OKC, Harden was playing more. He scored 17 points per game. He was a big part of the Thunder winning their **division**.

This time the Thunder played well in the playoffs. The team went 12–3 and made it to the NBA Finals. They lost the championship to the Miami Heat. Harden ended the season by winning the NBA's Sixth Man of the Year Award!

>>> Harden (right) and his teammates stand for the U.S. National Anthem after winning gold at the 2012 Olympics.

FACT

Harden won an Olympic Gold Medal as a member of Team USA in the 2012 London Olympics. Harden started every game, and the United States went 8–0.

CHAPTER FOUR
HARDEN TO HOUSTON

On October 27, 2012, the Oklahoma City Thunder shocked the basketball world. They traded Harden to the Houston Rockets as part of a six-player deal. He got to Houston less than a week before the start of the season. The Rockets gave their new guard a five-year contract worth $80 million.

Harden was finally a starter. He proved right away he was worth the money. He scored 37 points in his Rockets debut against the Detroit Pistons. Harden started 78 games for the Rockets and averaged almost 26 points per game.

The Rockets faced Oklahoma City in the first round of the 2012–13 playoffs. Harden played well against his old team. The Thunder beat the Rockets four games to two. Even though they lost, Rockets' fans were still excited. The team missed the playoffs three years in a row before Harden arrived. Now, thanks to The Beard, they were back!

>>> Harden brings the ball down the court during a 2012 Houston Rockets game.

After eight seasons in Houston, Harden became
one of the league's best scorers. In 2017–18, his offense
earned him his first NBA Most Valuable Player
(MVP) Award. He averaged more than 30 points
per game. That year, Harden led the Rockets to the
division title.

〉〉〉 Harden poses with
his MVP Award at the
2018 NBA Awards.

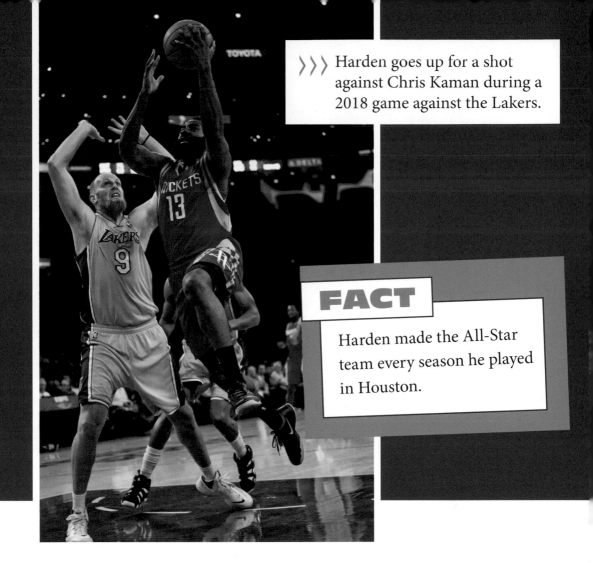

》》》 Harden goes up for a shot against Chris Kaman during a 2018 game against the Lakers.

FACT

Harden made the All-Star team every season he played in Houston.

Harden didn't slow down. He averaged 36 points per game in the 2018–19 season. On January 30, 2018, Harden became the only player in history to record a 60-point **triple double**. He was a scoring machine against the Orlando Magic. Harden added 10 **rebounds** to carry his team to a 114–107 win. He led the league, winning the scoring title every season from 2017–18 to 2019–20.

>>> Harden speeds past Utah Jazz forward Georges Niang during the 2019 NBA playoffs.

PLAYOFF POWER

Harden made the playoffs in his first 11 NBA seasons. Harden has put up more than 40 points in eight playoff games. One of his strongest performances came in the 2019 playoffs against the Utah Jazz. Harden finished with 32 points, 13 rebounds, and 10 **assists**. It was his third postseason triple double.

But in the biggest games of his playoff career, Harden has played poorly. In his last six **elimination games**, Harden has shot just 38 percent from the floor. He has also had about seven **turnovers** per game. Those numbers are part of why he never led the Rockets to the Finals.

CHAPTER FIVE
FUTURE NBA CHAMPIONSHIP?

Harden has never won an NBA title. Part of a player's legacy is how many championship rings he has won. Michael Jordan won six. Kobe Bryant finished his career with five, and LeBron James has four. Does Harden have to win a championship to be considered one of the greats? Many fans think so. Instead, his team was eliminated by the Los Angeles Lakers in the 2020 Western Conference Semifinals.

As a starter, Harden has failed to reach the NBA Finals. But even if he never wins a title, Harden will still be remembered as a superstar. Many NBA Hall of Fame players never won a title. Charles Barkley, Reggie Miller, and Patrick Ewing ended their careers with no championships.

>>> Harden beats Kyle Kuzma to the basket during a 2020 game against the Lakers.

NEXT STOP: BROOKLYN

After the 2019–20 season Harden asked the Rockets to trade him. When they didn't, he spoke out in the media. He said the team wasn't talented enough to win a championship. Harden was trying to force his way out of Houston, and it worked.

On January 14, he was traded to the Brooklyn Nets. Harden joined former Thunder teammate Kevin Durant in Brooklyn. Nets fans hope that together, they will bring an NBA Title to the Nets.

〉〉〉 Harden drives the ball against Orlando Magic's Cole Anthony.

TIMELINE

1989 James Harden is born on August 26 in Los Angeles, California.

2007 As a senior at Artesia High School, Harden is named a McDonald's All-American.

2007 Harden begins college at Arizona State University on a basketball scholarship.

2009 Harden is drafted in the first round of the NBA Draft by the Oklahoma City Thunder.

2010 Harden is named to the NBA All-Rookie Team.

2012 Harden is traded to the Houston Rockets.

2012 Harden wins a gold medal for the United States at the London Olympics.

2014 Harden is named to his first All-Star team.

2018 Harden is named the NBA's Most Valuable Player.

2020 Harden wins his third NBA scoring title in a row.

2021 Harden is traded to the Brooklyn Nets.

GLOSSARY

ASSIST (uh-SIST)—a pass that leads to a score by a teammate

ASTHMA (AZ-muh)—a disorder that makes it difficult to breathe

CHEMISTRY (KE-mis-tree)—how certain personalities interact

DEBUT (DAY-byoo)—a first showing

DIVISION (duh-VI-zhuhn)—a group of people or teams in a certain category for a competition

ELIMINATION GAME (i-li-muh-NAY-shuhn GAYM)—a playoff game where if a team loses, the series is over

NBA COMBINE (en-bee-AY KOM-byn)—an event where scouts and coaches judge the best college players in areas like speed and strength. It helps them decide who they want to draft

REBOUND (REE-bound)—the act of gaining possession of the ball after a missed shot

RECRUIT (ri-KROOT)— to ask someone to join a college team

ROOKIE (RUK-ee)—a first-year player

TRIPLE DOUBLE (trip-uhl-DU-buhl)—when a player reaches double digits in three of the following: points, rebounds, and assists

TURNOVER (TURN-oh-vur)—to lose possession of the ball

VARSITY (VAR-si-tee)—the main team representing a high school or college in a sport or other competition

READ MORE

Bryant, Howard. *Legends: The Best Players, Games and Teams in Basketball.* New York: Philomel Books, 2017.

Chandler, Matt. *Breanna Stewart: Pro Basketball MVP.* North Mankato, MN: Capstone Press, 2022.

Jankowski, Matt. *The Greatest Basketball Players of All Time.* New York: Gareth Stevens, 2020.

INTERNET SITES

NBA: James Harden
nba.com/player/201935/james_harden

NCAA: Men's Basketball
ncaa.com/sports/basketball-men/d1

Jr. NBA
jr.nba.com

INDEX